W9-AWQ-272

To the two Barbaras

Take the
IQ Challenge 2

Philip J. Carter & Ken A. Russell
Joint editors of the
MENSA PUZZLE GROUP JOURNAL

JAVELIN BOOKS
LONDON · NEW YORK · SYDNEY

First published in the UK 1987 by Javelin Books,
Artillery House, Artillery Row, London SW1P 1RT

Copyright © 1987 Philip J. Carter

Distributed in the United States by
Sterling Publishing Co., Inc.,
2 Park Avenue, New York, NY 10016

Distributed in Australia by
Capricorn Link (Australia) Pty Ltd,
PO Box 665, Lane Cove, NSW 2066

Typeset by Poole Typesetting (Wessex) Ltd
Printed in Great Britain by Robert Hartnoll, Bodmin

ISBN 0 7137 2000 X

CONTENTS

ACKNOWLEDGEMENTS

Thanks are due to the British Mensa Committee, under the chairmanship of Sir Clive Sinclair, for agreeing to the publication of this book, with special thanks to Secretary Jan Evans for the prompt and courteous way she dealt with our application. Thanks also to British Mensa's Executive Director, Harold Gale, for his support and to International Executive Director, Ed Vincent. No Mensa book should be without thanks to Mensa's Honorary President, Victor Serebriakoff, for his many years of dedicated work for Mensa. Thanks also to Dr Madsen Pirie, for allowing us use of some of his wise words from his column in the British journal, 'Mensa'. Special thanks to all members of Enigmasig for their support, regretfully space does not allow us to list them all, but we feel we have to mention, in particular, Cynan Rees, Maurice Sobell and Paul Perriman for a constant flow of contributions to the Enigmasig newsletter over a long period. Last, but certainly not least, a huge amount of thanks to Barbara Carter, not just for preparing the typescript with such expertise, and for spotting and correcting mistakes in several puzzles, but also to her and Barbara Russell for their continued enthusiasm, and support, for all our projects, and for their never ending optimism.

INTRODUCTION

In 1986 Mensa, the society for those with a measured IQ within the top two percent of the population, celebrated its Ruby Anniversary. Founded on the 2 October 1946, following a chance remark between two strangers, an Australian, Roland Berrill and an Englishman, Lancelot Lionel Ware, during a train journey through Surrey on a hot summer's day in August of the previous year, it has grown into an international worldwide organisation of some 80,000 members. Mensa means many things to many people and has been described as 'a very enjoyable social club', 'an ever widening circle of interesting and pleasing friends', 'a place of discovery', 'a diversity of people, their ideas and opinions', 'thought provoking and stimulating' and 'an intellectual round table without internal hierarchies or élites'. Being a round table society (the word *mensa* is Latin for 'table'), Mensa has no opinions and all its members are of equal standing, but inevitably they do have, and express, their own views on every possible subject and are encouraged to come together to form Special Interest Groups (SIGS). Mensa has many such groups devoted to subjects as varied as astrology, oriental cooking, ecology, computers, politics, shyness, space exploration and Egyptology, indeed if there is not already a group to suit one's own specialised interest, all that is necessary is to form such a group to attract members of a like mind.

This brings us to Enigmasig, the SIG devoted to the setting and solving of puzzles, and it is our involvement with this group which has inspired us to put together this compilation, which should provide an insight into the perplexing puzzle solving world of Mensa and the diverse range of puzzles which entertain and frustrate its members. Diversity is the keyword of our compilation, Kickself to Brainbender, Warm up to Wind up, all with a widely ranging degree of difficulty, and so that you can monitor your performance throughout we have allocated, to each puzzle, one of the following star ratings;

> * standard
> ** more challenging
> *** difficult
> **** appallingly difficult

The majority of puzzles are in the one and two star category, but there are four particularly fiendish brainbenders which we consider to be so complex as to warrant a four star rating. You will see that each puzzle is cross-referenced with two numbers, a question number (Q) and an answer number (A), which has enabled us to mix up the answers section so that there is no risk of seeing the next answer before tackling the puzzle.

We hope we have whetted your appetite for finding out more about Mensa. Puzzle solving is only a small fraction of the wide range of activities which take place within the society, but if you do apply for membership, and are successful, we hope that one day we will have the pleasure of welcoming you as a member of our own Special Interest Group, Enigmasig.

Variety is the spice of life and our aim in putting together this compilation has been to include as wide a selection of different types of puzzles and of as varying degrees of difficulty, as possible. Our first section is designed to limber up your mind for what is to follow, and, maybe, to give you some inkling of how our own devious minds work.

Good luck, and happy solving!

(a) What letters complete these sequences?   (See A108)

    * (i)   M, V, E, M, J, S, U, N, ?

    * (ii) C, D, I, L, M, V, ?

   ** (iii) P, W, E, L, G, A, ?

(b) What is the next letter in this sequence?   (See A66)

    * O, T, F, S, N, E, T, F, S, N, T, T, ?

(c) What vowels complete these sequences?   (See A17)

   *** (i) E, OAE, EO, EE, UE, IIO, ?

    ** (ii) UA, OA, UEA, EEA, UA, IA, ?

(d) Should the letter K go above or below the line?   (See A30)

   *
A			E F		H I	
	B C D			G		J

(e) Fill in the missing letters.   (See A42)

   *

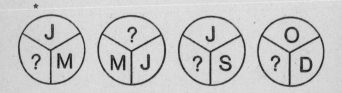

(a) Work out the missing numbers.   (See A44)

    * (i)   4, 9, 25, 49, 121, 169, 289, 361,
           ?, ?, 961

    * (ii)   97376, 7938, 1512, ?

    * (iii) 1, 4, 27, 256, ?

   ** (iv) 33278, 9436, 4278, 2996, ?

 *** (v)   22196, 4294, 988, ?

(b) Consider the number 7731.   (See A113)

Now continue the sequence –

 *** 153, 193, 197, 353, 413, 419, 793, 797, 813,
     819, ?, ?

(c) Find a reason for arranging these numbers into   (See A2)
groups of three.

  ** 127, 196, 361, 414, 428, 533, 565, 566, 693,
     761, 775, 961.

(d) Work out the missing number.   (See A126)

* (a) What do these words have in common?   (See A61)

    STUDIO, CALMNESS, FIRST, INOPERATIVE,
    DEFEND.

* (b) *DESTRUCTION* IS TO *RUIN* AS *INSTRUCTOR*
    IS TO: (See A16)

    TEACHER, TUTOR, TRAINER, COACH,
    EDUCATOR.

*** (c) Consider the following list of words: (See A20)

    RACK, ON, GAIN, RAGE, ROW.

    Now choose one of the following words to add to the list:

    HEDGE, WOOD, STORM, TRACK, MAID,
    WATER, MILK.

** (d) Fill in the missing letters and read clockwise (See A119)
    to find the eight-letter words:

(i)   (ii)   (iii)

** (a) A wheel is spun containing 10 red and 10 yellow equal segments. Above the wheel is an arrow. What are the chances that in any 10 consecutive spins the same colour will appear against the arrow? (See A80)

* (b) Eight bingo balls numbered from 1 to 8 are placed into a bag then drawn out at random, one by one, and the numbers written down to form an eight-figure number. What are the odds that the eight-figure number will divide by 9 exactly? (See A57)

* (c) If the man who always transgressed against divine or moral law was named Dennis, the girl who always felt unwell was named Delia, and the lady who had a thing of value was named Tessa, what was the name of the man who carried a bag of letters? (See A111)

* (d) Jim, Alf and Sid each win on the horses for three days running. The following are the nine amounts which the bookie paid out (starting with the largest amount through to the smallest amount). (See A93)

£65 – £52 – £47 – £39 – £26 – £23 – £21 – £15 – £12.

Jim won twice as much as Sid. What was the total winning amount for each man over the three days?

All the puzzles in this section consist entirely of diagrammatic representation. To solve them you have to apply your mind to each set of diagrams, comprehend the experience before you, and decide what logical patterns and/or sequences are occurring. The puzzles here are not ones of numeracy or literacy but are purely exercises of the mind, designed to test raw intelligence, free from the influence of prior knowledge.

We have shown several examples of the type of diagrammatic exercises used in intelligence tests – matrices, advanced matrices – conditions, but have devised all the exercises specially for this book, so that they are all original and not taken from actual intelligence tests.

Study the diagram and decide what logically should be the missing section from the choices given. (See A31)

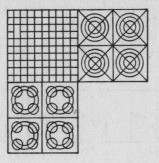

Choose from:

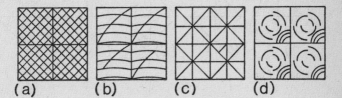

(a)   (b)   (c)   (d)

Find the next figure: (See A114)

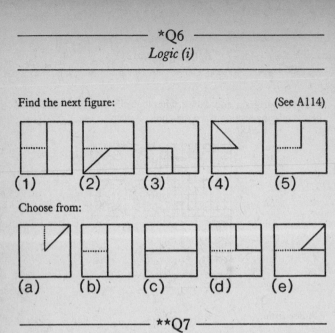

Choose from:

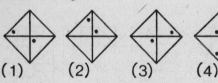

Find the next figure: (See A54)

Choose from:

Consider the three trominoes below: (See A88)

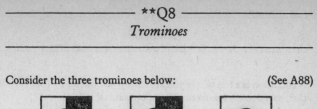

Now choose one of the following to accompany the above:

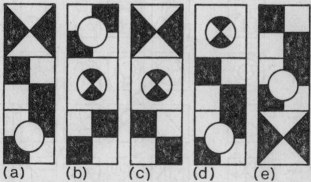

(a)   (b)   (c)   (d)   (e)

Conditions

A condition is a test where you are shown one box and (See A100) then asked to choose from a list of options which one other box meets the same conditions, e.g. which of the five boxes on the right meets the same conditions as the box on the left.

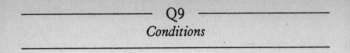

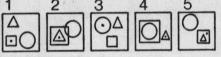

The answer is 3 because it is the only one where the dot is inside the circle. Now try the following (to increase the difficulty in A, B and E the dots are shown only in the left-hand box).

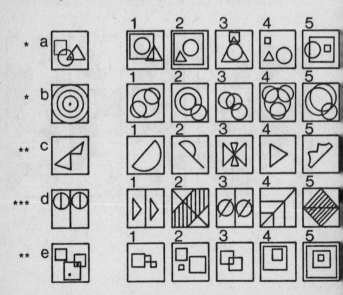

Look along each line horizontally, and then down each line vertically to find what, logically, should be the missing square.

(See A37)

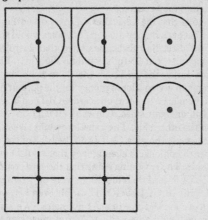

Choose from:

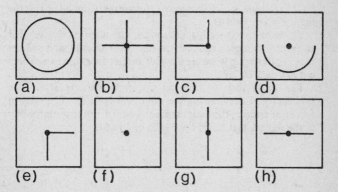

Man has always been a gambler. The urge to defeat the laws of probability is inherent in most people, although it was not until the 17th century, when Blaise Pascal, a French mathematician formulated the first rules relating to probability, that people were really aware that they existed.

It was in 1654 that the Chevalier de Méré asked Pascal why he lost when he bet even money that a pair of sixes would show once in 24 rolls of the dice. Pascal demonstrated that 24 rolls would be against the gambler, but 25 rolls could be slightly in his favour.

In America during the gold-rush era, there was a very ingenious gambling game that won a lot of money for the perpetrators. Three cards would be placed in a hat: one card GOLD on both sides, one card SILVER on both sides, one card GOLD on one side and SILVER on the other side. The gambler would take one card and place it on the table showing GOLD on the back of the card. Then he would bet the onlookers even money that GOLD would be on the reverse side. The reasoning being that the card could not be the SILVER/SILVER card therefore there were only two possibilities GOLD/SILVER or GOLD/GOLD. A fair even bet, or is it? The catch is that we are dealing in *sides* not cards. We start with six sides, three gold and three silver. We eliminate the SILVER/SILVER card and we can see one GOLD side. That leaves two GOLD and one SILVER unseen. Odds are therefore 2-1 on that the reverse side is GOLD.

The basic rule is really quite simple. Calculate the chances that an event will happen and then calculate the chances that it will not happen. Example: What are the odds against drawing a named card out of a pack of 52?

The probability of drawing the right card is 1/52. The probability of not drawing the right card is 51/52. The odds in favour of drawing the right card is the ratio of the first probability to the second, that is, 1/52 to 51/52, or 1 to 51.

Heads and Tails

(See A4)

A friend of yours is tossing a coin and you are betting him on the outcome. You bet on heads every time. Your unit stake is £1 per toss. You begin by betting £1 on the first toss. If you win, you again place £1 on the second toss but if you lose you double the stake to £2 then £4 and continue to double after every loss. After every win you revert to the £1 stake. After 100 tosses of the coin, heads has come down 59 times. How much profit are you making, assuming that the one-hundredth toss was heads?

Typist

(See A101)

A typist types four envelopes and four letters. She places the letters in the envelopes at random. What are the chances that only three letters are in their correct envelopes?

★★★Q13
Yarborough

(See A9)

A hand in bridge in which all 13 cards are a nine or below is called a Yarborough, after the second earl of Yarborough (d.1897), who is said to have bet 1000 to 1 against the dealing of such a hand. What, however, are the actual odds against such a hand? Was the noble lord onto a good thing?

★★Q14
Probability Paradox

(See A63)

Four balls are placed in a hat. One is yellow, one is blue and the other two are red. The bag is shaken and someone draws two balls from the hat. He looks at the two balls and announces that one of them is red. What are the chances that the other ball he has drawn out is also red?

*Q15
Lucky Card

(See A13)

In a competition each person receives a card with a number of rub-off pictures. One picture is marked loser, and only two pictures are identical. If the two pictures which are identical appear before the picture marked loser appears, then the competitor wins a prize.

There are 60 pictures on the card – what are the odds against winning?

**Q16
Snooker

(See A43)

The game of snooker is played with 15 red balls, a black, a pink, a blue, a brown, a green, a yellow, and a white ball, which is the cue ball. Apart from the reds, which form a triangle at the top of the table, and the white, each of the remaining six coloured balls must be placed on its own spot on the table.

Two novices were setting up their first-ever game. They knew where to place the red balls and the cue (white) ball, but hadn't a clue which coloured ball went on which spot so decided to guess and spot the balls anywhere. How many possible different ways are there of spotting the six coloured balls?

CROSSWORDS

On Sunday 21 December 1913 the first crossword puzzle appeared in the *New York World*. It was devised by Liverpool-born Arthur Wynne, who called it a Word Cross Puzzle. That very first puzzle has since been reproduced exactly in several publications, but what we have done here is to create a completely new puzzle, using Arthur Wynne's original grid, but with an entirely different set of clues and answers. This tribute to Arthur Wynne is our first crossword puzzle in this set.

Word Cross Puzzle

Based on first crossword by Arthur Wynne.   (See A1)

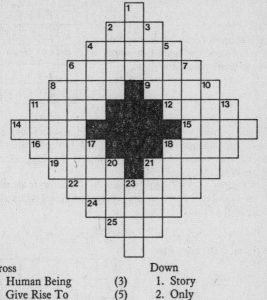

Across

2. Human Being (3)
4. Give Rise To (5)
6. Assembled (7)
8. Animal (4)
9. Vivacity (4)
11. Actor's Part (4)
12. Falsehoods (4)
14. Greek Letter (4)
15. MarshPlant (4)
16. Adorn (4)
18. Adjacent (4)
19. Page (4)
21. Imitates (4)
22. Parts of Coat (7)
24. Parts of Body (5)
25. Not High (3)

Down

1. Story (4)
2. Only (4)
3. Knob (4)
4. Expose (4)
5. Explain (4)
6. Spacious Buildings (7)
7. Milk Suppliers (7)
8. Inn (5)
10. Requires (5)
11. Colour (3)
13. Look with Eyes (3)
17. Vegetable (4)
18. Spill Out (4)
20. Tumbled (4)
21. Profess (4)
23. Made of Ebony (4)

Magic Word Square

(See A81)

T	E	P	I	D
E	L	U	D	E
P	U	P	I	L
I	D	I	O	T
D	E	L	T	A

This is a sample of a 5×5 magic square, so called because the same five words can be read both across and down.

Magic-word squares become rarer as the number of letters increases. An 8×8 square has been compiled, but so far not a 9×9 or 10×10, and we doubt if one is possible in the English or any other language.

This example is a 7×7 magic square. All the answers are seven-letter words and read both the same across and down, when placed correctly in the grid.

Clues (In no particular order)

Devour Greedily

False to his Allegiance

Lamp

Settles

Stricter

One who enters Profession

Eccentric

Answers run in the direction of compass points.   (See A137)

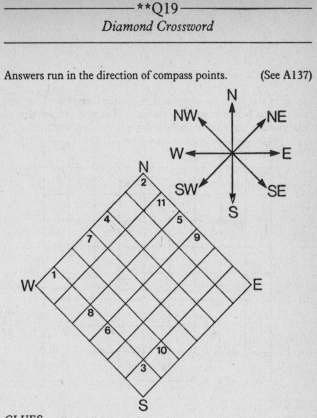

CLUES

1.E.	Palatable Liquids	5.W.	Exist
1.S.E.	Musical Piece	5.S.	Pain
1.N.E.	Harsh	6.N.	Before
2.S.	Errors	6.E.	Consumed
2.S.E.	Rubs Out	7.E.	Animal Doctors
3.N.E.	Spies	7.S.	Vehicle
4.E.	Age	8.E.	Midday
4.S.	Volcano	9.S.	Money
4.S.W.	Evenings	10.N.E.	Males
4.N.E.	Sooner Than	11.S.E.	Burns to the Ground

Criss-Cross

(See A40)

Answers run from the lower number in the direction of the next highest number and end on that number. The next answer starts on that number and runs to the next highest number, and so on.

1	5							4
10			13			12		7
	17						15	
							14	
				16				
11		8				9		6
3								2

CLUES

1. Expressed in Pictures (9)
2. Pair of Eye Glasses (9)
3. Tending to Expand (9)
4. Bring About (8)
5. Kidney Shaped (8)
6. Small Quantity (7)
7. Covered (7)
8. Slobber (5)
9. Lazily Reclining (7)
10. Hot Springs (7)
11. Exchanging for Money (7)
12. Pleased (4)
13. Given Medicine (5)
14. Beaded Moisture (3)
15. Used to be (4)
16. Dash (4)
17. Incline Head (3)

Nursery Rhyme Crossword

(See A25)

Complete the crossword, using the eight clues contained in the narrative below. Having·solved the clues, place the answers in the correct position in the grid.

Doctor Foster who was a person skilled at operating, and of great standing posture, went to Gloucester by devious and roundabout ways, in a violent storm which had a rotary motion, on a dark overcast day. Whilst studying some aimless scrawls he stepped in a no longer used quarry right up to his middle and was not up to the occasion.

Insert the 26 letters of the alphabet into each grid once   (See A103)
only. Only one word is common to both grids.

CLUES (no particular order/grid)
Ready Tongued
Fold or Thickness
Approach
A Mineral
Act Craftily
Nest in Rank
Moisture
Vault of Heaven
Addict
Foot Covered
Annoy
Leather Strip
Touchy
Falsehood
Shoots

Grid One

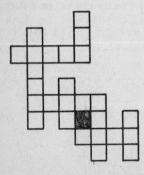

Grid Two

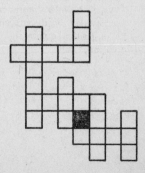

Here are five connected 5×5 magic squares. Answers (See A59) are all five-letter words and in each of the five grids read the same both across and down.

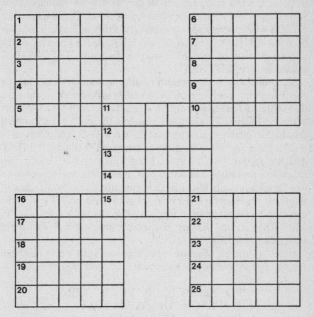

CLUES

1. Faded
2. Sky Blue
3. Money
4. Made Mistakes
5. Actions
6. Swap
7. Made Angry
8. Excuse
9. Sum Owed
10. Shortens
11. Express
12. Teacher
13. Make Amends
14. Medicine
15. Set Upright
16. Shot at Billiards
17. Pains
18. Makes Purchases
19. Colour
20. Composition
21. Vagabond
22. Runner
23. Sharp
24. Gives Out
25. Force

CRYPTOGRAMS

Cryptographers have at their disposal so much information on things like letter and word frequency that they will find the task of decoding the messages in this section extremely simple. Knowledge is continually being updated in the fields of letter frequency, word frequency, most common word endings, word beginnings, double-letter frequency, and so on. For example, the order in which letters appear most frequently in English today is ETAOINSRHLDCUMFPGWYBVKXJQZ; the order in which they appear most often at the beginning of a word is TAOSIWHCB and at the end ESDTNRYO.

So, armed with such a wealth of information, how does one go about decoding a cryptogram? The easiest to deal with are the ones that contain a four-letter word that begins and ends with the same letter, eg. FGHF. This is almost certainly the word THAT, which should then enable you to discover the word THE, and now you're well on your way to solving the cryptogram. If the word THAT does not appear, then try to work out what might be the letter E, single-letter words – usually A or I, and a repeated three-letter-word ending, usually ING (the most common three-letter ending in English). Also look for other obvious words such as AND; the most common two-letter word in English – OF, double letters (EE, FF, LL, OO, RR, and SS are the most common); and four-letter endings such as LESS and NESS.

Here's a little bit of nonsense to illustrate what we've just been saying. You should be able to decode it in about two minutes:

'FLOP LOPY PLOP?' YOWS TWEE.
'PLU KEOP LOP', YOWS TUG.
'IL PLOP LOP,' YOWS TWEE.
'PLOPY PLOP PLUG'.   (See A3)

The majority of cryptograms are straightforward simple types, where each letter of the alphabet is substituted for another, and there is only one message to be decoded. But what if the sender of the message wishes to convey a further message within the same cryptogram? This is done by the addition of keywords, which may be hidden in either the plain or the keyed text. As all the cryptograms which appear in this section have keywords or keyed phrases, we can show how these are uncovered by means of the following comment from Oliver Hardy, which he made to explain why he thought people found the L & H partnership so funny. (There is a further quotation keyed 5-2-4-8 by Henry Ward Beecher.)

G LZOKK GI BRK SOPRZKO BO BOHO KM PMFXWOIOWD ZQWGVO GQ OAOHD BRD. SZI WGVO SRPMQ RQN OLLK BO KOOFON IM SO RSMZI XOHTOPI IMLOIJOH — SZI QMI KM LMMN RXRHI.

This is simple substitution cryptogram, where one letter of the alphabet has been substituted for another, and is therefore deciphered in the usual way to arrive at the answer.

I GUESS IT WAS BECAUSE WE WERE SO COMPLETELY UNLIKE IN EVERY WAY. BUT, LIKE BACON AND EGGS, WE SEEMED TO BE ABOUT PERFECT TOGETHER — BUT NOT SO GOOD APART.

To find the keyed quotation place the code text in juxtaposition to the plain text, thus:

```
(PLAIN TEXT)  A B C D E F G H I J K L M N O P Q R
(CODE TEXT)   R S P N O T L J G   V W F Q M X   H
(PLAIN TEXT)  S T U V W X Y Z
(CODE TEXT)   K I Z A B   D
```

As nothing appears yet which might look like a message, arrange the code text alphabetically in juxtaposition to the plain text:

```
(CODE TEXT)   A B C D E F G H I J K L M N O P Q R
(PLAIN TEXT)  V W   Y   M I R T H S G O D E C N A
(CODE TEXT)   S T U V W X Y Z
(PLAIN TEXT)  B F   K L P   U
```

Usually the keyword or, in this case, the keyed quotation, contains the only letters which do not appear in alphabetical order. By inspecting the plain text you may usually easily pick out where the alphabet appears in orderly succession and thus isolate the keyword letters. Above we see A to Y in order, thus suggesting the keyed quotation is contained in the letters MIRTHSGODECN. Because letters cannot be repeated in simple cryptograms the fun now begins if the keyed quotation repeats letters. It is therefore necessary to use your imagination to make sense of the message. In this case the answer is MIRTH IS GOD'S MEDICINE.

The addition of keywords has several purposes in addition to the practical one of sending an additional message which may escape the attention of an interceptor. It gives the compiler an opportunity to comment on the coded material, which is usually a quotation, and possibly display his own wit, or lack of it, and it adds an extra dimension to the puzzle.

Now try to decode the following cryptograms. Each letter of the alphabet is substituted by another, each cryptogram is in a different code, and each contains a keyword or phrase.

*Q24
Cryptogram (i)

Message keyed, 10-2-4-6 (See A34)

SNL NQGCF SHZC T MHTK GN JNY GSHG LSCF JNY SHZC

CDTETFHGCK GSC TEWNMMTODC, LSHGCZCI ICEHTFM,

SNLCZCI TEWINOHODC, EYMG OC GSC GIYGS?

KNJDC

*Q25
Cryptogram (ii)

Message keyed, 4-3-4 (See A94)

ME MR SQAHQ EA ZPQJ ELPE HO QOON RAYMEFNO EA VMQN

AFDROYGOR. BODLPBR ME MR QAE RA HOYY SQAHQ ELPE

HO QOON RAYMEFNO EA VMQN AFD VOYYAHR OGOQ ELO

RPGMAFD MR NORUDMTON PR DOPULMQW ZPQSMQN

ELDAFWL ELO HMYNODQORR.

LPGOYAUS OYYMR

★★Q26
Cryptogram (iii)

One word keyed, 12   (See A92)

HDHJKJOT KUL ALOAHKJNO NS H AUNMK AUHMY AUNWQ,

SMNX H QULHY HOR QUJYYF QUNYYLM NO H PJT PIHQW

PINQW.

D. A. TJIPLMK

(KUL XJWHRN)

★★Q27
Cryptogram (iv)

Message keyed, 5-2-10   (See A86)

JIXRSJK SH LH GLHC LH SX NIIUH. GZGFCXRSJK XLUGH

NIJKGF XRLJ CIY GBEGPX. SQ LJCXRSJK PLJ KI AFIJK,

SX ASNN MI HI; LJM LNALCH LX XRG AIFHX EIHHSONG

VIVGJX.

VYFERC'H NLA

'Listen, I don't mind you presenting taxing problems, BUT, do they have to be such frustratingly simple solutions? For the record, I hold you personally responsible for the bruises I inflicted on myself after seeing the solution to those groups of numbers each totalling 1000. Do you realise that all the raw unharnessed brainpower failing on that one could possibly run a nuclear reactor for a year at least?

'P.S. Please send me a photograph of yourself superimposed on a dartboard.'

So wrote one Mensa member recently after failing to solve one particular Kick-Self puzzle.

Each month a Kick-Self puzzle appears in *Mensa*, the Journal of British Mensa with a small prize for the first correct entry drawn out. You will be amazed at the trouble some members will take to submit solutions. We have had instances of solutions posted by special delivery at a cost exceeding the prize on offer, but the classic story is of the member who, armed with what he thought was the correct solution, cycled to the puzzle editor's home in Kent and arrived in the early hours of the morning. He had pedalled furiously all the way from the Isle of Dogs in Essex, a journey of some three hours, but was told, on arrival, that the answer he was proudly clutching was, in fact, the wrong solution!

This was my old telephone number.   (See A10)
What does it remind you of?

(314) 159 – 2654

Base to explorer at the South Pole: (See A83)

'What's the temperature?'
'Minus 40°' said the explorer.
'Is that Centigrade or Fahrenheit?' asked base.
'Put down Fahrenheit,' said the explorer. 'I don't expect it will mattter.'

Why did he say that?

Where would you place 9 and 10 to keep the sequence   (See A91)
going?

1 2   6
———————————————
   3 4 5   7 8

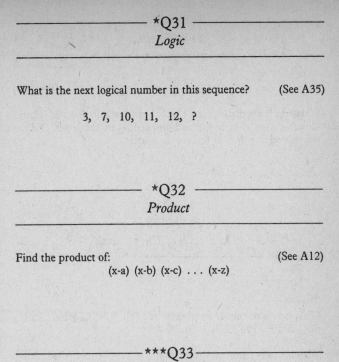

--------------- ⋆Q31 ---------------
Logic

What is the next logical number in this sequence?   (See A35)

3, 7, 10, 11, 12, ?

--------------- ⋆Q32 ---------------
Product

Find the product of: (See A12)
(x-a) (x-b) (x-c) . . . (x-z)

--------------- ⋆⋆⋆Q33 ---------------
Calculate It

Why does $(12570 + 0.75) \times 16 \div 333 =$ An animal?   (See A117)

39

(See A14)

I floated a lump of metal in a plastic bowl in a bath of water. Then I took the lump of metal out and dropped it into the water. Did the water level rise, fall, or remain the same?

──────── **Q35 ────────
The Barrel of Rum Puzzle

(See A136)

'This barrel of rum is more than half full,' said Charlie. 'No it's not,' said Harry. 'It's less than half full.'

Without any measuring implements how could they easily determine who was correct? There was no lid on the barrel and no rum was taken out.

(See A99)

Fill in the missing numbers:

4	7	8	3	8	5
6	5			7	4
8	1	8	6	2	
3	6	5	8	7	6
	7	2	6	3	7
8	4	7	4	7	5

―――――――――――★★★Q37―――――――――――
Palindrome

(See A53)

Change the position of *one* number only to make this a palindromic
sequence:

1, 4, 2, 9, 6, 1, 5, 10, 4

(See A33)

This is a true incident. See if you can figure out what actually happened.

Our golf club car park slopes steeply from south to north and the cars park in a vee-shape facing north (down-hill), as shown in the diagram.

Recently two friends arrived for a four-ball and parked in spaces C and F. About two hours later, whilst they were halfway through their round, the club secretary went onto the course to tell them that the car in space F had just rolled forward into the one in space C.

Both cars were in perfect order, had no defects, and no one or nothing had pulled or pushed either car or had tampered with them in any way. What is the explanation?

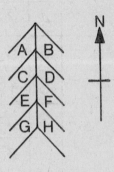

(See A19)

Two strangers enter a pub. The publican asks them what they would like. First man says, 'I'll have a bottle of stout,' and puts 50p down on the counter. Publican: 'Guinness at 50p, or Jubilee at 45p?' First man: 'Jubilee'. Second man says, 'I'll have a bottle of stout,' and puts 50p on the counter. Without asking him the publican gives him Guinness. How did he know what he required?

(See A116)

Man calls to waiter in the restaurant, 'There's a fly in my tea'. 'I will bring you a fresh cup of tea,' says the waiter. After a few moments the man calls out, 'This is the same cup of tea!' How did he know?

(See A11)

Study the numbers in each horizontal line and then decide what, logically, should be the missing numbers.

3 3 1	2 3 1 1	1 2 1 3 2 1

2 3 3	1 2 2 3	1 1 2 2 1 3

1 2 1	1 1 1 2 1 1	

———— ***Q42 ————
Ad Nauseam

(See A104)

What letter completes this sequence?

AEEOEEIEUE?

ANAGRAMS GALORE

Do you find solving anagrams as 'INCOMPREHENSIBLE' as solving a 'PROBLEM IN CHINESE'? Do you know a 'ONE WORD' anagram for 'NEW DOOR'? 'NOR DO WE'!

Anagrams were invented by the Greek poet Lycophon in AD 280. Originally an anagram was simply a word which when reversed formed another word. For example, ROOM/MOOR, or TIDE/EDIT. The word, 'anagram' is derived from Greek: 'ANA' means 'backwards' and 'GRAMMA' 'a letter'.

The best anagrams are those where the rearranged letters bear some relationship to the original word or name; for example, the letters of the word 'SOFTHEARTEDNESS' can be rearranged to form the phrase 'OFTEN SHEDS TEARS'.

For hundreds of years compilers have tried to find hidden meanings in rearranging the names of famous people. Some of our favourites are: 'I'LL MAKE A WISE PHRASE' (WILLIAM SHAKESPEARE), 'ON THEN, O SAILOR' (HORATIO NELSON), 'FLIT ON CHEERING ANGEL' (FLORENCE NIGHTINGALE) and 'OUR BEST NOVELS IN STORE' (ROBERT LOUIS STEVENSON). Politicians too inevitably find their names being rearranged into appropriate phrases. Depending on your point of view, 'MARGARET THATCHER' is either 'THAT GREAT CHARMER' or 'MEG THE ARCH TARTAR'; 'RONALD REAGAN' is 'LOAN ARRANGED'; and the former British prime minister 'WILLIAM EWART GLADSTONE' becomes 'WILD AGITATOR MEANS WELL'.

Before you tackle the host of anagrams that follow we will leave one particularly tricky little teaser with you. Rearrange the letters of the words 'ROAST MULES' to form a single 10-letter word. It is a common English word, with which everyone is familiar, but it is surprisingly very difficult to find (see A22).

--------------------------------- **Q43** ---------------------------------
Anagrams

All these are one-word anagrams: (See A60)

(a)   EASTER EGG   (f)   BORDELLO

(b)   IS A CHARM   (g)   ADMIRER

(c)   REMOTE   (h)   INTO MY ARM

(d)   OPEN CLAIM   (i)   THERE WE SAT

(e)   HOTEL SUITE   (j)   RESTFUL

--------------------------------- *****Q44** ---------------------------------
Swop Round

(See A132)

Change the numbers to letters to find three 9-letter words:

$$1 \quad 2 \quad 3 \quad 4 \quad 5 \quad 6 \quad 7 \quad 8 \quad 9$$

$$2 \quad 3 \quad 1 \quad 4 \quad 5 \quad 6 \quad 7 \quad 8 \quad 9$$

$$8 \quad 9 \quad 3 \quad 1 \quad 2 \quad 4 \quad 5 \quad 6 \quad 7$$

Anagram Phrases

(See A8)

Each word or phrase in quotation marks is an anagram of another word. The solution bears some relationship to the original.

(a) 'UP CLOSE' 'TRIFLING'   (7/8)

ANSWER: '_____' '_____'

(b) 'EMIT GRUNT' through 'MOUTH CASE'   (9/9)

ANSWER: '_____' through '_____'

* (a) All American presidents: (See A89)
    - (i)   OH! GOING? GREAT NEWS
    - (ii)   RAM BALL ON CHAIN
    - (iii) BOTH HERE ROVER
    - (iv) WIND OR OWLS WOO
    - (v)   LODGE CIVIC LOAN
    - (vi) O DO REVERSE THE TOOL
    - (vii) A FOOLER SENT LINK OVERLAND

** (b) All well-known writers: (See A78)
    - (i)   KEN SCARES CHILD
    - (ii)   REASON ANN IT'S HARD CHINS
    - (iii) LOB NET OR CHATTER
    - (iv) NEW SMILE ESSENTIAL
    - (v)   A BELL CHARMS
    - (vi) TO STEER NOON SILVER BUS
    - (vii) SHAME MARE MUST GO

(See A36)

You must enter each room once only in a continuous route and spell out a 15-letter word. You may enter the corridor as many times as you wish.

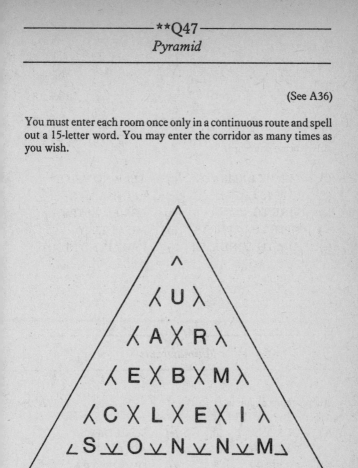

(See A85)

Antigrams are anagrams in which the letters of a word are reorganized to form a word or phrase meaning the opposite. Answers are one word.

(a)	I LIMIT ARMS	(f)	TEAR NO VEILS
(b)	IS IT LEGAL? NO	(g)	ARCHSAINTS
(c)	FINE TONIC	(h)	ARE ADVISERS
(d)	NICE TO IMPORTS	(i)	MORE TINY
(e)	AIM TO CONDEMN	(j)	CARE IS NOTED

───────── *Q49 ─────────
Animalgrams

All anagrams of animals.   (See A32)

(a)	CORONA	(e)	SOMEDAY
(b)	PAROLED	(f)	ALPINES
(c)	RETIRER	(g)	ORCHESTRA
(d)	LESIONS	(h)	CALIFORNIA†

†two words

In each of the following unscramble the letters to find a word.
There are no two adjoining letters in the same shape.

   * (a) 11-letter word.   (See A5)

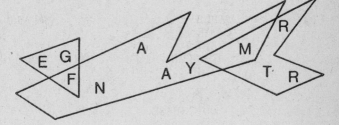

   ** (b) 12-letter word.   (See A118)

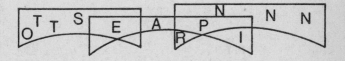

   *** (c) 14-letter word.   (See A62)

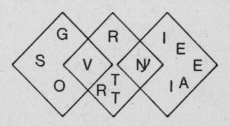

Anagram Themes

In each set below arrange the 14 words in pairs so that each pair is an anagram of another word or name. The seven words produced will have a linking theme. For example, if the words 'DIAL' and 'THAN' were in the list they could be paired to form an anagram of 'THAILAND' and the theme would be countries.

(a)   AMPLE   (See A56)
        CAME
        CARE
        CENTRE
        CHIN
        COIN
        CORD
        CREASE
        MORE
        RAP
        SHAKE
        THE
        TO
        TRY

(b)   FEED   (See A39)
        FRAIL
        GAIN
        GRIN
        GRIP
        HEAT
        HERS
        LAG
        LAST
        LOVE
        PANS
        TRADE
        TRAMP
        WAIT

It is interesting how some numbers have their own individual characteristics.

With some numbers it is possible to tell if they are a factor of a large number without having to do a division calculation. Examples of such numbers are 3, 9 and 11. With 3 and 9 all that is necessary is to total up the digits. If their sum is divisible by 3 or 9 then the number itself is divisible by 3 or 9, e.g. the sum of the digits 3912 is 15, which divides by 3 exactly. Therefore, the number 3912 or any combination of these digits also divides exactly by 3. Similarly the digits 497286 total 36, which divides by 9, so the number 497286 or any combination of these digits also divides exactly by 9.

The test for 11, which is not so well known, is to see if the separate sums of alternate digits are equal, e.g. the number 746218 is divisible by 11 exactly, when read either forward or backward, because $7+6+1 = 4+2+8$.

There is also a way of finding out if a number is divisible by 7 or 13. The system is the same for both 7 and 13 and it is to split the number into groups of three starting from the end and insert alternating minus/plus signs. For example, $587932 \times 7 = 4115524$ and $4 - 115 + 524 = 413$; therefore, because 413 is divisible by 7, so is 4115524; similarly $896712 \times 13 = 11657256$, so $11 - 657 + 256 = -390$ and as 390 is divisible by 13, so is 11657256.

Another interesting number is 37, because when multiplied it very often produces a palindromic number or, if not palindromic, a number which will divide by 37 when read forward or backward. The reason for this is simply that it is a third of the number 111, and we have illustrated its palindromic qualities later.

Somehow all the numbers mentioned above – 7, 9, 11, 13, 3, 37, (111) – seem to come together in the magic six digits 142857. This is the number which fascinated Charles Lutwidge Dodgson (1832-98), who was a lecturer in mathematics at Oxford from 1855 until 1881, but is better known as Lewis Carroll.

By dividing 1 by 7 we get the cyclical number 0.142857142857 and by multiplying together $3 \times 9 \times 11 \times 13 \times 37$ we get the same recurring digits 142857. Taking the same six digits Carroll discovered some fascinating characteristics.

$$142857 \times 1 = 142857$$
$$142857 \times 2 = 285714$$
$$142857 \times 3 = 428571$$
$$142857 \times 4 = 571428$$
$$142857 \times 5 = 714285$$
$$142857 \times 6 = 857142$$

The six digits always stay in the same order but move round each time so that each digit occupies each of the six positions. When multiplied by 7 the result is a row of six nines. If you add the first and last three digits the result each time is 999.

It was almost certainly this number that inspired the Mad Hatter's Tea Party, which illustrates the idea of cyclic order:

'Let's all move one place on'.

Like ourselves Carroll loved tinkering with words and numbers and inventing and solving puzzles. We don't know if he experimented further with his magic number, but we have done so, and by dividing each of the numbers in TABLE ONE by 3, 9, 11, 13, 37 and 111 in turn have arrived at the following results:

Table Two (÷3)	Table Three (÷9)	Table Four (÷11)
47619	15873	12987
95238	31746	25974
142857	47619	38961
190476	63492	51948
238095	79365	64935
285714	95283	77922

Table Five (÷13)	Table Six (÷37)	Table Seven ÷111)
10989	3861	1287
21978	7722	2574
32967	11583	3861
43956	15444	5148
54945	19305	6435
65934	23166	7722

Except for TABLE THREE, it can be seen that all the numbers in the other tables are linked in some characteristic way.

In TABLES ONE, TWO, FOUR and FIVE the sum of the digits of each number is 27. In TABLES SIX and SEVEN the sum of the digits of each number is 18. In TABLES FOUR and FIVE the middle digit of each number is 9. In TABLE FOUR the sum of the vertical second and fifth row of figures is 27. In fact, these vertical rows contain the magic digits 124578 but not in their cyclic order. In TABLE SEVEN the numbers are the same as TABLE FOUR without the centre digit 9.

All this would have surely interested Carroll considerably, and no doubt he would have approved of the following curious little puzzle which we have devised to illustrate the palindromic qualities of the number 37.

**Q52

The Magic '37'

(See A90)

If the digits 1 – 9 are placed in the grid as follows:

4	6	2
7	1	9
8	5	3

a total of 16 different numbers will be formed if each horizontal, vertical and corner-to-corner line is read both forward and backward.

Rearrange the digits 1 – 9 in the grid in such a way that if each of the 16 three-figure numbers are extended to form a palindromic six-figure number (e.g. 462264 or 264462) then each of those 16 six-figure numbers will divide exactly by 37.

Nine G-R-R-RID

(See A6)

Place the digits into the grid in such a way that every horizontal and vertical line when read both forwards and backwards, and also the sum of the digits of every horizontal and vertical line, can be divided by nine exactly.

1, 1, 1, 2, 2, 2, 2,

3, 3, 4, 4, 5, 5, 6,

7, 7, 7, 7, 7, 7,

8, 8, 9, 9, 9.

Elevenses

Place the digits into the grids so that each horizontal and vertical line is divisible by 11 exactly, when read either forwards or backwards. Remember, no multiplication or division is necessary. All you need to do is ensure that the alternate digits in each horizontal and vertical line when added together equal the same; for example, 5148, i.e. 5 + 4 = 1 + 8.

(a)   (See A112)

1, 1,

3, 3, 3, 3, 3,

4, 4, 5, 5,

6, 6, 8, 8, 9.

(b)   (See A102)

1, 1, 1,

2,

3, 3, 3, 3, 3,

4, 5, 5, 6, 7, 8, 9.

(a)   (See A38)

These two four-figure numbers share a feature in common
with only one other four-figure number. What is the feature
and what is the other number?

3600,   5776

(b)   (See A67)

These two four-figure numbers share a feature in common with
only one other four-figure number. What is the feature and what is
the other number?

2025,   9801

ODD ONE OUT

One of our very good friends in Enigmasig, Cynan Rees, once sent us an odd-one-out puzzle with a difference. He gave us a list of six words and asked us to make out a case for each of the words being the odd one out for a different reason. The words he presented us with were:

ABORT
ACT
AGT
ALP
OPT
APT

Can you find a reason for each of the words being the odd one out? (For answer see A45.) This puzzle is a fine example of the pitfalls which compilers must try to avoid. Hopefully all the puzzles which follow in this section will have just one clear reason why one only of the options given is the odd one out.

(See A18)

Which one of these sentences is the odd one out?

(1) FRIENDSHIP LINGERS UNTIL THE END.

(2) LOVERS STROLL UNDER THE STARS.

(3) HEAVEN ALWAYS REPAYS PERFECTION.

(4) THE UPROAR BEGINS AGAIN.

──────── **Q57 ────────
Words

In each of the following which is the odd one out?

(a)   (See A115)   (b)   (See A122)

DEBT	SING
AIM	RECORD
KNOW	TEAR
TWO	REBEL
SCENE	WIND
AEON	

(See A41)

Which of these figures is the odd one out?

(a)   (b)   (c)   (d)   (e)

———— ***Q59*** ————
Spot The Dot

(See A138)

One of the dots in this circle is an intruder. Which one?

(See A55)

An intelligence test where you are shown a number of boxes and asked to choose the one which is different is called 'Classification'. Which one of the following boxes is the odd one out?

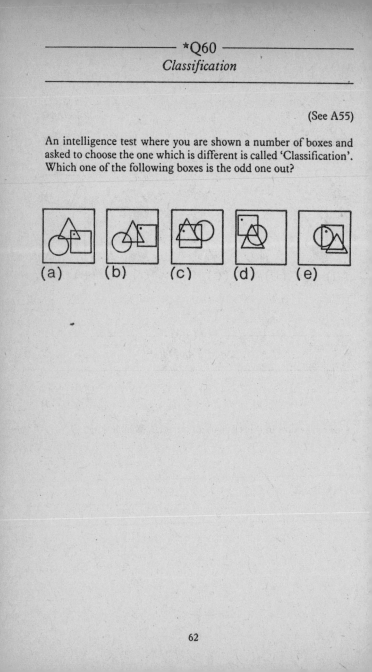

(a)   (b)   (c)   (d)   (e)

(See A75)

Which of these four crosses is the odd one out?

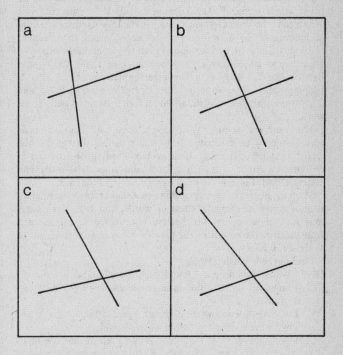

The English language, the most commonly spoken language in the world, has evolved from an awkward native dialect, the tongues of various invaders and the importation of other foreign words after the expansion of the British Empire.

The basic element of the English language is Teutonic, or German, and the dialects spoken by the various English and Saxon tribes which overran England during the fifth to seventh centuries belonged to the West Germanic group of the Indo-Germanic family of languages. To a basis of Anglo-Saxon words the Norman Conquest added many Norman-French words of Latin origin to which were added many more words from Latin during the Renaissance. Finally, with the great expansion of the British Empire, words were imported from countries such as India, and other terms introduced by sailors and travellers from all parts of the world.

The result is a language consisting of some half a million words and spoken by an estimated 400 million people throughout the world. Because of the way it has evolved the English language is rich in alternative words such as 'work' and 'labour', 'friendly' and 'amiable' and is one of the most expressive of all tongues.

Mensans never tire of discovering new delights about the English language and its treasure chest of words, and below are some examples of wordplay which have entertained and fascinated Enigmasig members during the past few months. (For the answers to these see A15.)

Find in the English language:

(a) A word containing three adjacent pairs of double letters.
(b) Two words which although antonyms are pronounced exactly the same.
(c) The longest word which does not repeat letters.
(d) The shortest word to contain all five vowels.
(e) Two commonly used words, one of 11 letters and one of 13 letters, which start and finish with the same three letters in the same order.
(f) A 12-letter word having a 2:1 vowel to consonant ratio.
(g) The only word which has the letters 'GNT' in succession.
(h) An 8-letter word which forms another word when reversed.
(i) Four words containing all five vowels in the correct forward or reverse order.

Spiral clockwise round the perimeter and finish at the centre square to spell out the nine-letter words. Each word commences at one of the four corner squares.

* (a) (See A110)

** (b) (See A79)

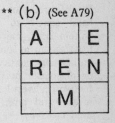

* (c) (See A27)

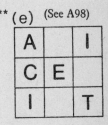

*** (d) (See A51)

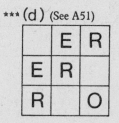

** (e) (See A98)

65

⋆Q63
Wot! No Vowels

(See A21)

Work from the top left-hand square to the bottom right, moving from square to square horizontally, vertically or diagonally to find five words. Every letter in the grid must be used once only.

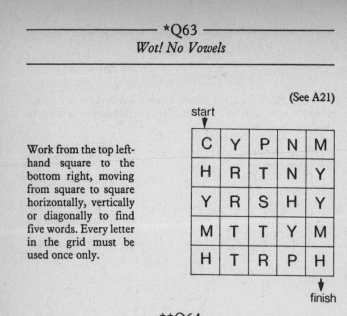

start ▼

C	Y	P	N	M
H	R	T	N	Y
Y	R	S	H	Y
M	T	T	Y	M
H	T	R	P	H

▼ finish

⋆⋆Q64
Alphabet

Use the 26 letters of the alphabet once each to complete these words.

ABCDEFGHIJKLM
NOPQRSTUVWXYZ   (See A73)

1. — A – E
2. L – – – R I – –
3. Z – – E
4. – O U – –
5. – O Y
6. – Y – E
7. – E – R –
8. – – A – I – –
9. E – I – –

Pair Words

(See A68)

Here are two lists of words.

Each word in List A has two possible pair words in List B.
Each word in List B has two possible pair words in List A.

There are two possible solutions.
Pair a word from each list until you have 10 pairs.

List A	*List B*
SEVERN	TRACTOR
ARROW	RIVER
TURRET	BULL'S-EYE
FARM	BOW
YARBOROUGH	TANK
SAND	CARDS
YEW	CASTLE
VEHICLE	BANK
RIPARIAN	WOOD
JACK	BRIDGE

(See A123)

What have all the answers to the following clues in common?

1. DOCTRINE
2. FEELER
3. HOLDING FAST
4. FISH
5. OFFER
6. GAME
7. FRAME
8. THIN
9. MEANING
10. FIT FOR HABITATION

(See A77)

The following words are a logical progression:

THAT
DOCUMENTATION
MEANDER
GRAVY
EMBANKMENT
JUBILEE

Which is next – EXTERMINATION, OCCUPATION, GRAMMAR, or ZOO?

(See A70)

Each horizontal and vertical line includes the consonants of a word which can be completed by adding a number of 'U' vowels. The two-figure number at the end of each line indicates the number of consonants and 'U' vowels, e.g. 2-1 indicates two consonants and one 'U' vowel.

	1	2	3	4	5	6	7	
1	R	S	J	T	G	R	K	2·1
2	S	S	C	F	S	C	C	4·2
3	C	C	P	M	P	B	S	5·2
4	S	G	S	L	P	F	Z	2·2
5	C	R	B	S	M	S	C	5·3
6	M	C	C	F	L	S	C	4·3
7	T	T	P	S	T	F	H	3·1
	4·1	3·2	3·1	4·1	3·1	3·1	4·1	

Each letter in the grid is used once only and all letters must be used. (The consonants to be used in each line are not necessarily in the correct order or adjacent.)

CLUES

Across	Down
1. CONTAINER	1. ROOF SUPPORT
2. NORTH AFRICAN DISH	2. SPIRITUAL TEACHERS
3. BE OVERCOME	3. HORN OF CRESCENT
4. BANTU	4. MATERIAL
5. FEMALE DEMON	5. LIGHT SHOE
6. CLOUD	6. BIRD
7. STRIKE GOLF BALL	7. PART OF LATHE

69

(See A120)

Each of the sentences below contains, in the correct order, the letters of a word that is opposite to the meaning of the sentence, e.g. *CLOSE TO BOILING* = COOL.

Find the words:

(a) A HAVEN OF LOVELINESS
(b) NOT FOR SOME TIME OR MAYBE NEVER
(c) FROZEN, NOT OFF THE SHELF
(d) A GREAT EFFORT AND STILL FRESH ENOUGH TO DO IT OVER AGAIN
(e) PUT YOUR EFFORT IN SHIFTING IT TOWARDS US
(f) SEW IT VERY TIGHTLY TOGETHER
(g) A LOT OF COMPANY FOR ME
(h) HATED OR REVILED
(i) READ IN COMPLETE SILENCE TO YOURSELF
(j) INDELICATE, UGLY AND UNCULTURED
(k) TRUSTY, EVER SINCERE AND HONEST
(l) NEW AND INEXPERIENCED MEMBER OF OUR BODY AND PROFESSION
(m) RUN ALONG SPEEDILY IN THE RACE
(n) NOW STALE AND VERY WORN

(See A72)

Answers are all six-letter words. Pair up two sets of three letters to form the answer.

CLUES
1. SEAMEN'S CHURCH
2. ANIMATING SPIRIT
3. ALLIGATOR
4. KEPT IN THIRD PERSON'S CUSTODY
5. INSOLENT PRIDE
6. WATCH A GAME OF CARDS
7. FASHIONABLE
8. POROUS LAVA
9. FULL OF CHINKS
10. SMALL PERFUMED BAG
11. SWOLLEN
12. WHIMSICAL NOTION
13. SHELL MONEY
14. SLUGGISHNESS
15. GENTLE BREEZE
16. NECKLACE OF TWISTED METAL

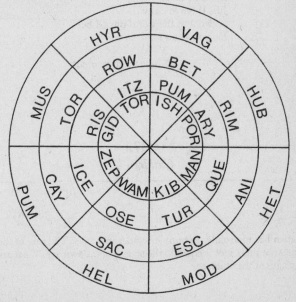

Mathematics may be defined as the subject in which we never know what we are talking about, nor whether what we are saying is true.

Bertrand Russell

**Q71
Number Rhyme

(See A74)

> If my three were a four,
> And my one were a three,
> What I am would be nine less
> Than half what I'd be.
>
> I'm only three digits,
> Just three in a row,
> So what in the world must I be?
> Do you know?

(Whole number used)

***Q72
Children

(See A106)

A man has nine children born at regular intervals. The sum of the square of their ages is equal to the square of his own age. What are the ages of the children?

(See A23)

This field, 112 m × 75 m, can be split up into 13 square plots.
Fill in the dimensions.

All dimensions are in whole metres.

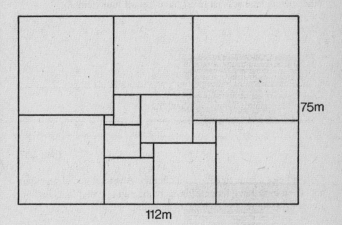

112m

75m

Not to scale

(See A71)

A sneak thief had been at work in the classroom. When the pupils returned from lunch 80 per cent had lost a pencil, 85 per cent had lost a pen, 74 per cent had lost a ruler and 68 per cent had lost a rubber.

What percentage at least must have lost all four items?

—— *Q75* ——
Sisters

(See A87)

Coincidence seems to run in our family. Although my sisters Pam and Fran each have five children, twins and triplets, Pam had her twins first whereas Fran had triplets first.

I saw Pam the other day, and she remarked that the sum of the ages of her children was equal to the product of their ages. I pointed out that although interesting this was not unique, as Fran could say exactly the same about her children.

How old are my sisters' children?

(See A65)

Arrange the following digits, 1 – 2 – 3 – 4 – 5 – 6 – 7 – 8 – 9, to form
a single fraction that equals one third.

(See A28)

Without changing the order of the digits form a calculation equal to
100. Only four plus and/or minus signs can be inserted between the
digits.

$$9 \quad 8 \quad 7 \quad 6 \quad 5 \quad 4 \quad 3 \quad 2 \quad 1 \quad = \quad 100$$

(See A109)

Without changing the order of the digits insert four plus signs, one
division sign and three minus signs between them to make the
calculation correct.

$$9 \quad 8 \quad 7 \quad 6 \quad 5 \quad 4 \quad 3 \quad 2 \quad 1 \quad = \quad 0$$

(See A49)

When the Roman army needed to punish a large number of men, every tenth soldier was executed – hence the word 'decimate'.

You are one of a band of 1,000 mutinous pirates, captured and tied to numbered posts arranged in a circle.

The first is to be executed, then each alternate pirate, until one remains, who will go free.

Which number post would you choose?

———————————— **Q80 ————————————
Decimal Points

(See A26)

In this addition sum, only one decimal point is in its correct position. Alter four of the decimal points to make the sum correct.

$$
\begin{array}{r}
36.7 \\
1874.5 \\
109.6 \\
14.8 \\
\hline
383.11
\end{array}
$$

Fifty-seven matchsticks are laid out to form the sum below, which is obviously incorrect.

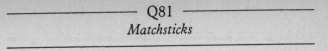

But by removing *two* matchsticks it is possible to make the sum correct:

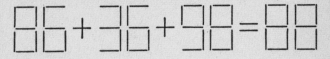

** (a) Now the same sum is again laid out, but this time remove *eight* matchsticks to make the sum correct. (Do not disturb the matchsticks already laid out, apart from the eight to be removed.)

(See A130)

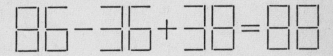

* (b) Now an incomplete sum. This time *add 18* matchsticks to make the sum correct. (Do not disturb the matchsticks already laid out.) This one is a kick-self.

(See A52)

QUOTATIONS

Among the 10 quotations in this section we have selected three by
William Shakespeare, including the first one, an acrostic.

(See A121)

Solve the clues, place each letter in its appropriate position in the grid, and a Shakespeare quotation will appear.

	LING	(7)	2F	8B	2C	1E	12C	3F	18D		
	AVAILS ONESELF OF	(4)	13F	5F	12A	14E					
	REMAINS	(7)	15D	15B	10F	7B	19F	17F	7A		
	HAUGHTY	(6)	15C	21E	7E	15A	10B	13E			
	AMOUNTING TO	(10)	17B	16F	2B	14F	7D	4F	20E	14B	5B	5A
	MUSCLE CRAMP	(7)	14C	7C	12E	10E	13B	9D	18F		
	SEEKS JUSTICE FROM	(4)	19D	17D	6F	17A					
	ENTRANCE	(9)	20B	3C	16E	9A	11D	6A	16D	7F	6E
	A CARDINAL NUMBER	(4)	3C	1B	12B	19C					
	GREAT HAPPINESS	(8)	1A	9C	17C	6B	1C	4B	3D	4E	
	BE OF VALUE	(5)	9E	8F	18E	1D	13A				
	FAINTS	(6)	19E	16A	2A	4D	2D	8A			
	LIFT UP	(7)	10D	6D	16C	18C	14D	11C	17E		
	FOAM	(5)	11A	3A	11B	1F	18B				
	DOES WRONG	(7)	12F	3B	20A	13C	20F	8D	20C		
	CUT WITH AXE	(3)	2E	9F	11E						
	OF THE THIGH	(7)	13D	3E	8C	19A	5C	19B	14A		

Two In One

In each of the following, two quotations are squashed together. All the letters are in the correct order. Find the two quotations. To assist, the authors' names follow the quotations but have been squashed together in the same way.

(See A29)

* (a) AALLLKLLENOARNWINLEDGGIESBIUSTBRUE
TCREOMELMLBECRATNICOEN
SPOCLRAATETOS

(See A76)

** (b) TOYOEUHARVETRWOEAISRSHEHARBUOTHMS
IDANTESOFOFTORHEGIVQUEESDTIVIOINNE
SPPOURGPEEON

Find the Quotations

In each of the following find the starting point, fill in the missing letters, and a quotation will appear. Then rearrange the missing letters to find the author/originator of the quotation.

*(a) Author (5 letters) (See A58) *(b) Author (6 letters) (See A82)

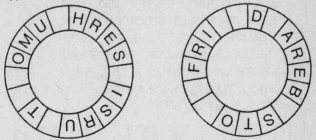

*(c) Originator (6,6) (See A64)

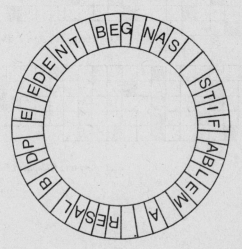

I'll Make a Wise Phrase

(See A24)

Place each word in the correct position in the correct grid and two Shakespeare quotations will appear.

> A, A, ART, BIRD, BUT, DAY, DID,
> EVER, FAULTS, GIVE, GODS, HAUNCH,
> HUMANITY, IN, LIFTING, MAKE, MEN,
> NEVER, OF, OF, RARER, SINGS, SOME,
> SPIRIT, STEER, SUMMER, THE, THE,
> THOU, TO, UP, US, US, WHICH,
> WILL, WINTER, YOU.

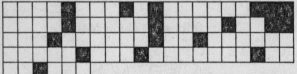

King Henry IV, Part 2, IV. iv

Antony and Cleopatra, V. i. 31

'It is quite a three-pipe problem.' – Sir Arthur Conan Doyle.

In this section we have chosen what we consider to be some of the most difficult problems, or, we should say, puzzles, in the book. Some time ago in 'Mensa' (the magazine of British Mensa), Dr Madsen Pirie defined the difference between puzzles and problems. A puzzle, he said, is set by another person, and it has a solution, or more, which is already known by that person. It is a puzzle to ask 'Which three-digit number has the most factors?' (see A96) or 'What is the lowest number (apart from 0 and 1) that is a square number, a cube number, and a number to the 4th power, 5th power and 6th power'. (See A7). A problem, on the other hand, arises in life. It is not set artificially and there is not an answer already known by someone else. There is no right answer; some solutions may be better than others.

While both puzzles and problems bring their rewards some may prefer one to the other. Certainly the successful solution of a problem achieves a worthwhile goal and perhaps the major benefit to be obtained from tackling puzzles is that they stretch and exercise the mind and enable you to tackle the real problems of life with renewed vigour and confidence.

(See A135)

Arrange the following into groups of three:

ARQUEBUS
ATOLL
BOARD
CANAL
DOOR
FIELD
FLINTLOCK
GUN
ISLET
KEY
NOTE
STONE

(See A69)

Which is the odd one out and why?

CHIS
DENC
FRAP
PERL
PORL
SPAD

(See A128)

A 2½ in. square card is thrown at random onto a tiled floor. What are the odds against its falling not touching a line?

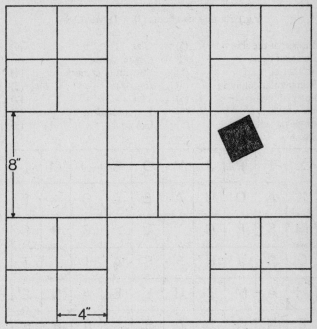

You should assume that the pattern repeats over a large area.

Letter Search

(See A131)

Answers will be found in letter order in the grid. Use every letter in the grid once each only:

(e.g.) Elastic-sided boots (7) = JEMIMAS

Disease of the skin	(5)	Clan	(4)
Dance of death	(7)	Cotton fabric	(9)
Mother-of-pearl	(5)	Student of archery	(11)
Rectangular column	(8)	Inert gas	(5)
Force of men	(5)	Veil	(7)
Chip basket	(6)	Lettered board	(5)
Angle of building	(5)	Colour	(5)
Shrub	(6)		

X	T	P	J	Y	O	S	N	M	O
X	A	O	U	A	E	E	O	A	E
M	S	P	C	I	N	P	C	P	S
O	R	J	H	P	S	A	I	I	T
M	A	M	B	U	L	E	A	N	E
Z	N	Q	L	A	S	A	A	R	H
E	U	I	K	U	A	N	E	S	S
L	O	I	P	T	E	P	L	V	E
L	I	U	T	I	T	E	V	E	E
A	R	T	A	E	N	E	E	S	N

How many triangles are there in each of the following figures? The number of triangles increases in each figure. The first figure is a warm-up.

*(a)   (See A107)   ***(b)   (See A95)

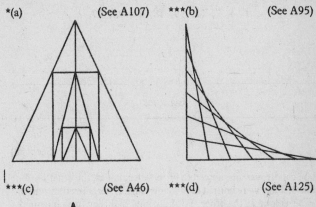

***(c)   (See A46)   ***(d)   (See A125)

 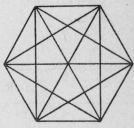

───────── ***Q91 ─────────
Sequence

(See A97)

What is the next number in this sequence, and why?

1, 4, 7, 11, 15, 18, 21, 24, 27, ?

───────── ***Q92 ─────────
Candles

(See A50)

One candle was guaranteed to burn for six hours, the other for four hours. They were both lit at the same time. After some time one was twice as long as the other. For how long had they been burning?

───────── ****Q93─────────
Amicable Numbers

(See A134)

These are rare numbers. They are	?	?
pairs of numbers where the sum of	1184	1210
the factors of one is equal to the	5020	5564
other and vice versa.	6232	6368
What are the two numbers in the	10744	10856
first pair? They are both under 300.	17926	18416
	9437056	9363584

Regular puzzle solvers may have noticed that from time to time we are influenced by one of our great puzzlist heroes, Charles Lutwidge Dodgson (Lewis Carroll). Throughout his life Carroll was fascinated with inventing and solving puzzles, and these are sprinkled throughout his popular works. Perhaps his most popular and lasting puzzle invention is 'Doublets', which you will know as the puzzle where the task is to change one word into another in several stages. Before you tackle the final section, which includes an example of another of Carroll's favourite type of puzzle, 'Double Acrostic', we will leave you with one particular 'Doublet' puzzle, which remained unsolved by Mensa members until very recently, when several solutions were put forward. The puzzle is how to change 'MENSA' into 'WORLD' by altering just one letter each time. For the Mensa solution (seven stages) see A133. See if you can do it in less!

M E N S A

- - - - -

- - - - -

- - - - -

- - - - -

- - - - -

- - - - -

W O R L D

Family Way

(See A84)

My two uncles and five cousins were all born on different days of the week. Uncle Alan was born on a Friday and his daughters, my cousins Judith and Mary, were born on a Monday and Saturday respectively. My other uncle, Paul, was born on a Sunday and his eldest son, my cousin Richard, was born on a Thursday. His other sons, Roy and Terry, were born on the two remaining days of the week; but which one was born on a Tuesday and which one was born on a Wednesday?

───────── *Q95 ─────────
The Meeting

(See A129)

The man from the country at the top of the Himalayas came by plane to meet the man from the Far East who was wearing a chain round his neck. What was the weather when they met the man from the Middle East?

(See A105)

Each couplet provides the clue to a word. When you have solved
them, read down the first and last letters of the five words to reveal
two further words.

> Very brief a note to play,
> Liquid measure either way.
>
> Here's a title I suspect,
> Turkey, Sir, yes with respect.
>
> Just an idea or a fancy,
> Opinion, belief or view you can see.
>
> Listen closely hear the clue,
> You paid attention, good for you!
>
> Now a line, or coalition,
> Revolve around it with precision.

(See A124)

Commence at the centre square and work from square to square horizontally, vertically and diagonally to find eight ships. Every square is used once only. Finish at the top right-hand square.

H	T	I	E	J	C	H	→
E	G	E	R	T	U	T	
R	Y	A	F	A	N	E	
T	C	N	✳	G	K	K	
H	A	K	O	I	R	R	
T	E	L	O	R	F	E	
R	S	P	T	A	W	L	

(See A47)

Find the missing square:

FR	NE	TO
TE	FE	SN
ET	OE	

Choose from:

(a) TE (b) ZF (c) XN (d) OK

(e) PC (f) KR (g) SX (h) MX

(See A48)

Each horizontal and vertical line contains the jumbled letters of a country. Find the 20 countries. Every letter is used, but only once each.

A	A	I	I	R	N	D	I	I	G
R	N	I	I	U	U	M	P	I	E
K	A	T	R	Y	A	U	A	E	R
K	A	A	E	Y	N	U	D	E	O
T	A	L	N	A	A	A	N	M	O
L	R	A	E	I	G	R	N	A	I
M	Y	J	L	N	I	A	A	T	T
I	N	F	A	A	P	B	J	T	A
P	M	I	N	I	C	A	A	H	S
P	P	Y	G	U	B	R	C	C	S

(See A127)

We were determined that this book should have a happy ending, and if the sound of laughter isn't happy then we don't know what is. All these words are connected with humour.

(a)   – H – M – Y
(b)   – L – P – T – C –
(c)   – A – T – R
(d)   – A – I – A – U – E
(e)   – U – F – O – E – Y
(f)   – U – L – S – U –
(g)   – O – U – A – I – Y
(h)   – P – O –
(i)   – A – I – A – E
(j)   – A – I – E
(k)   – A – C –
(l)   – A – T – O –
(m)   – O – X
(n)   – O – E – Y

ANSWERS

We hope you managed to arrive at many of the correct answers and that you derived a great deal of satisfaction and pleasure from doing so. We have ensured that all the answers are fully explained, so that for those which you were unable to crack, you will obtain a clear idea of what you should have done to come up with the correct solution. We hope that, in some way, we have added to your store of knowledge and we feel sure that by tackling our compilation you will have increased your puzzle-solving (and hopefully problem-solving) capacities.

Finally, why not learn more about Mensa and how to take the Mensa Entrance Test by writing to one of the addresses below? From our own experience we can assure you that if you qualify for membership the rewards you obtain will far outweigh the effort involved.

British Mensa Ltd.,   American Mensa Ltd.,   Australian Mensa,
Bond House,   2626 E14 Street,   16 Elliot Avenue,
St. John's Square,   Brooklyn,   Carnegie,
Wolverhampton,   N.Y. 11235.   Victoria 3163.
WV2 4AH.

A1 (Q17) Across: 2. Man, 4. Begot, 6. Paraded, 8. Hare, 9. Elan, 11. Role, 12. Lies, 14. Beta, 15. Reed, 16. Deck, 18. Side, 19. Leaf, 21. Apes, 22. Sleeves, 24. Elbow, 25. Low.
Down: 1. Saga, 2. Mere, 3. Node, 4. Bare, 5. Tell, 6. Palaces, 7. Dairies, 8. Hotel, 10. Needs, 11. Red, 13. See, 17. Kale, 18. Spew, 20. Fell, 21. Avow, 23. Ebon.

A2 (Q2c) $428 + 533 = 961$, $566 + 127 = 693$, $361 + 414 = 775$, $565 + 196 = 761$.

A3 (Cryptograms, Introduction) 'What hat's that?' said Bill.
'The flat hat', said Ben.
'Oh, that hat,' said Bill.
'That's that then.'

A4 (Q11) You win £59. You will always win the same number
            of units that heads comes down in the sequence,
            providing the final toss is heads.

A5 (Q50a) Fragmentary.

A6 (Q53)   52938
            49617
            78453
            97722
            21177

A7 (Brainbenders for Mentalathletes, Introduction) 2^{60}.

A8 (Q45) (a) Couples Flirting (b) Muttering through
            Moustache.

A9 (Q13) In a pack of 52 cards there are 32 cards of nine or
            below. The chance that the first card dealt is one of
            the 32 is $\frac{32}{52}$, the second card $\frac{31}{51}$ etc.
            The chance of all 13 being favourable is $\frac{32}{52} \times \frac{31}{51} \ldots \frac{20}{40}$
            or $\frac{1}{1828}$.
            The odds were strongly in Lord Yarborough's
            favour.

A10 (Q28) It is pi to nine decimal places: 3.141592654.

A11 (Q41) 121 – 111211 – 311221. Each number describes the
            previous number, i.e. 121 then 1-1, 1-2, 1-1, then 3-
            1s, 1-2, 2-1s.

A12 (Q32) At some time during the calculation you will be
            multiplying by (x-x), which equals 0, therefore the
            product will be 0.

A13 (Q15) 2/1. The number of pictures on the card does not
            affect the odds.

A14 (Q34) When the metal was taken out of the bowl, the bowl
            displaced less water, so the water level fell by an
            amount corresponding to the volume of water which
            would have the same weight as the metal. When the
            metal was immersed in the water, it displaced its own
            volume of water and the water level rose. The

amount it rose corresponded to the volume of the metal, very much less than the volume of an equal weight of water. Hence the net result was a fall in water level.

A15 (Words, Introduction)
     (a) Bookkeeper.
     (b) Raised/Razed.
     (c) Uncopyrightable or Dermatoglyphics.
     (d) Euphoria.
     (e) Underground, Entertainment.
     (f) Onomatopoeia.
     (g) Sovereignty.
     (h) Desserts/Stressed.
     (i) Facetious, Abstemious, Uncomplimentary, Subcontinental.

A16 (Q3b) Tutor: its letters are contained in instructor in the correct order as with destruction/ruin.

A17 (Q1c) (i) IOE. They are the vowels extracted from the colours of the rainbow – red, orange, yellow, green, blue, indigo, violet.
(ii) AUA. They are the vowels extracted from the days of the week – Sunday, Monday, Tuesday, Wednesday, Thursday, Friday, Saturday.

A18 (Q56) 2: The initial letters of the others spell out musical instruments – flute, harp, tuba.

A19 (Q39) He puts down 4 × 10p and 2 × 5p coins. If he had required Jubilee he would have put down 4 × 10p and 1 × 5p coins.

A20 (Q3c) Maid. All words can be prefixed with BAR to form another word.

A21 (Q63) Crypt, Rhythm, Tryst, Hymn, Nymph.

A22 (Anagrams Galore, Introduction) Somersault.

A23 (Q73)

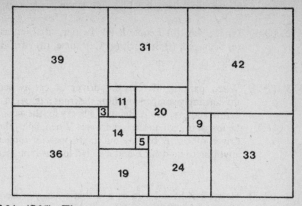

A24 (Q85) Thou art a summer bird which ever in the haunch of
winter sings. The lifting up of day.
A rarer spirit never Did steer humanity;
but you, Gods,
will give us Some faults to make us men.

A25 (Q21) Across: Disused, Tornado, Unequal, Sunless.
Down: Detours, Surgeon, Stature, Doodles.

A26 (Q80)   3.67
            18.745
             1.096
            14.8
            ―――――
            38.311

A27 (Q62c) Circulate.

A28 (Q77) $98 - 76 + 54 + 3 + 21 = 100$.

A29 (Q83a) All knowledge is but remembrance – (Plato).
            All learning is but recollection – (Socrates).

A30 (Q1d) Above the line. Straight letters go above; curved
letters below.

A31 (Q5) (d) So that each corner sub-square of each of the four main sections has a line missing.

A32 (Q49) (a) Racoon, (b) Leopard, (c) Terrier, (d) Lioness, (e) Samoyed, (f) Spaniel, (g) Carthorse, (h) African lion.

A33 (Q38) When parking his car the driver of car F had unknowingly stopped touching the front bumper of a car parked in space E. Being in a hurry for the game, he forgot to pull on the handbrake. When, later, the driver of car E backed out there was no longer anything to hold car F and it rolled forward into car C.

A34 (Q24) How often have I said to you that when you have eliminated the impossible, whatever remains, *however improbable,* must be the truth?

(Conan) Doyle

Message keyed: (ELMNTARYDWSO) – Elementary, my dear Watson.

A35 (Q31) 17 (seventeen): All numbers containing only 'E' vowels.

A36 (Q47) Incommensurable.

A37 (Q10) Looking across, the curved lines merge and the straight lines disappear. Looking down, the reverse happens. The missing square is, therefore, (f).

A38 (Q55a) They contain their square root, i.e. 3600, 5776; 2500 is the other four-figure number sharing this feature.

A39 (Q51b) Ptarmigan (Tramp Gain), Starling (Grin Last), Wagtail (Wait Lag), Fieldfare (Feed Frail), Shoveler (Love Hers), Partridge (Grip Trade), Pheasant (Heat Pans).

A40 (Q20) 1. Pictorial, 2. Lorgnette, 3. Explosive, 4. Engender, 5. Reniform, 6. Modicum, 7. Muffled, 8. Drool, 9. Lolling, 10. Geysers, 11. Selling, 12. Gald, 13. Dosed, 14. Dew, 15. Were, 16. Elan, 17. Nod.

A41 (Q58) (c) All the others are symmetric about a horizontal axis, i.e. they appear the same turned upside down.

A42 (Q1e) F.A.A.N. They are the initials of the months of the year.

A43 (Q16) 720, i.e. 6! or $6 \times 5 \times 4 \times 3 \times 2 \times 1$.

A44 (Q2a) (i) 529; 841. They are the squares of progressive prime numbers.
(ii) 10. i.e. $9 \times 7 \times 3 \times 7 \times 6 = 7938$. $7 \times 9 \times 3 \times 8 = 1512$. $1 \times 5 \times 1 \times 2 = 10$.
(iii) 3125. i.e. 5^5. The sequence is 1^1, 2^2, 3^3, 4^4, 5^5.
(iv) 2574. It is the odd numbers from the previous number multiplied by the even numbers, i.e. 99×26.
(v) 792. It is the square numbers from the previous number multiplied by the remaining numbers, i.e. 9×88.

A45 (Odd One Out, Introduction)
Abort (it is five letters long.)
Act (Last letter cannot be placed first to form another word.)
Agt (Not an actual word.)
Alp (Does not end in 'T'.)
Opt (Does not start with 'A')
Apt (Not in alphabetical order with rest.)

A46 (Q90c) 105.

A47 (Q98) SX: Each square contains the first and last letters of the numbers one to nine positioned in such a way so as to form a magic square where each horizontal, vertical and corner-to-corner line totals 15.

A48 (Q99) Lines across: India, Peru, Turkey, Kenya, Malta, Nigeria, Italy, Japan, Spain, Cyprus.
Lines down: Mali, Panama, Fiji, Niger, Iran, Cuba, Burma, Canada, Haiti, Togo.

A49 (Q79) 976. Take 2 to the power which gives the lowest number above 1000, which is $2^{10} = 1024$.
Formula $= 1024 - \{(1024-1000) \times 2\} = 976$.

A50 (Q92) Three hours. After x hours,
$$A \text{ had burned } \tfrac{x}{6} \text{ leaving } \tfrac{6-x}{6}$$
$$B \text{ had burned } \tfrac{x}{4} \text{ leaving } \tfrac{4-x}{4}$$
But after x hours, A was twice as long as B.
Therefore $\tfrac{6-x}{6} = \tfrac{2(4-x)}{4}$ Therefore x = 3.

A51 (Q62d) Reservoir.

A52 (Q81b)

A53 (Q37) 1, 4, 9, 6, 1, 5, 10, 4, 2., Now change to Roman numerals: I, IV, IX, VI, I, V, X, IV, II.

A54 (Q7) (b) The outer dot moves clockwise, first by one position, then two positions, then three, etc. The inner dot moves anti-clockwise, first by one position, then two positions, then three, etc.

A55 (Q60) (e) It is the only one where the dot is inside the circle.

A56 (Q51a) Policeman (Ample Coin), Mechanic (Came Chin), Teacher (The Care), Carpenter (Rap Centre), Doctor (To Cord), Secretary (Try Crease), Shoemaker (Shake More).

A57 (Q4b) Certainty. The sum of the digits 1-8 is 36. Any number divides by 9 exactly when the sum of its digits also divides by 9 exactly. It does not matter in which order the balls are drawn out as the sum will always be 36.

A58 (Q84a) Too much rest is rust – (Walter) Scott.

A59 (Q23) 1. Paled, 2. Azure, 3. Lucre, 4. Erred, 5. Deeds, 6. Trade, 7. Riled, 8. Alibi, 9. Debit, 10. Edits, 11. State, 12. Tutor, 13. Atone, 14. Tonic, 15. Erect, 16. Masse, 17. Aches, 18. Shops, 19. Sepia, 20. Essay, 21. Tramp, 22. Racer, 23. Acute, 24. Metes, 25. Press.

A60 (Q43) (a) Segregate, (b) Charisma, (c) Meteor, (d) Policeman, (e) Silhouette, (f) Doorbell, (g) Married, (h) Matrimony, (i) Sweetheart, (j) Fluster.

A61 (Q3a) They each contain three adjacent consecutive letters of the alphabet, e.g. *stu*dio.

A62 (Q50c) Tergiversation.

A63 (Q14) There are six possible pairings of the four balls: red/red, red(1)/yellow, red(2)/yellow, red(1)/blue, red(2)/blue and yellow/blue. We know the yellow/blue combination has not been drawn out. This leaves five possible combinations remaining, therefore the chances that the red/red pairing has been drawn out are 1 in 5.

A64 (Q84c) All bad precedents began as justifiable measures – Julius Caesar.

A65 (Q76) $\dfrac{5832}{17496}$

A66 (Q1b) T. They are initials of odd numbers; one, three, five, etc.

A67 (Q55b) Their two halves added together equal their square root, i.e. 2025 (20 + 25 = 45) and 45^2 = 2025. The other four-figure number sharing this feature is 3025.

A68 (Q65)

Solution 1		*Solution 2*	
Vehicle	– Tank	Vehicle	– Tractor
Turret	– Castle	Turret	– Tank
Sand	– Bank	Sand	– Castle
Riparian	– River	Riparian	– Bank
Severn	– Bridge	Severn	– River
Yarborough	– Cards	Yarborough	– Bridge
Jack	– Wood	Jack	– Cards
Yew	– Bow	Yew	– Wood
Arrow	– Bull's-eye	Arrow	– Bow
Farm	– Tractor	Farm	– Bull's-eye

A69 (Q87) Spad. The remainder are the first three letters of a country followed by the first letter of its capital. Chile-Santiago, Denmark-Copenhagen, France-Paris, Peru-Lima, Portugal-Lisbon.

A70 (Q68) Across: 1. Jug, 2. Cuscus, 3. Succumb, 4. Zulu, 5. Succubus, 6. Cumulus, 7. Putt.
Down: 1. Truss, 2. Gurus, 3. Cusp, 4. Stuff, 5. Pump, 6. Ruff, 7. Chuck.

A71 (Q74) Add the percentages together, which gives $80 + 85 + 74 + 68 = 307$ among 100 pupils. This gives 3 losses each and 4 losses to 7 pupils. The least percentage is, therefore, 7.

A72 (Q70) 1. Bethel, 2. Animus, 3. Cayman, 4. Escrow, 5. Hubris, 6. Kibitz, 7. Modish, 8. Pumice, 9. Rimose, 10. Sachet, 11. Turgid, 12. Vagary, 13. Wampum, 14. Torpor, 15. Zephyr, 16. Torque.

A73 (Q64) 1. Wave, 2. Limerick, 3. Zone, 4. Dough, 5. Joy, 6. Pyre, 7. Zebra, 8. Qualify, 9. Exist.

A74 (Q71) Half of 'What I'd be' must be a whole number. 'What I'd be' must be an even number. 'What I am' cannot end in 1. There are four possible arrangements of the three digits.

	(a)	(b)	(c)	(d)
'What I am'	1?3	13?	31?	?13
'What I'd be'	3?4	34?	43?	?34

'What I am' is 'Nine less than half what I'd be'.
So ('What I am' + 9) × 2 = 'What I'd be'.
Examination shows that only 'A' fits the bill and 'What I am' must be 183.

A75 (Q61) (c) It is the only cross that will not fit snugly inside a 1in square.

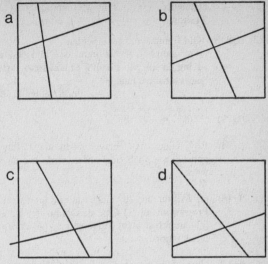

A76 (Q83b) To err is human, to forgive, divine.　　　(Pope).
You have two ears; hear both sides of the question.
　　　　　　　　　　　　　　　　　　(Spurgeon)

A77 (Q67) Grammar. Each word starts with the letter whose position in the alphabet coincides with the number of letters in the preceding word, i.e. 'THAT' has four letters; therefore the next word starts with the fourth letter in the alphabet – D.

A78 (Q46b)
　　(i)　Charles Dickens　　(ii)　Hans Christian Anderson
　　(iii Charlotte Bronte　　(iv)　Tennessee Williams
　　(v)　Charles Lamb　　　(vi)　Robert Louis Stevenson
　　(vii) Somerset Maugham

A79 (Q62b) Enumerate.

A80 (Q4a) One in 1024. Each spin is an even chance; i.e. 1 in 2. To repeat 10 times is 1 in 2^{10}.

A81 (Q18) Nestles   Lantern
            Entrant   Engorge
            Strange   Sterner
            Traitor

A82 (Q84b) Old friends are best – Selden.
The complete quotation reads: Old friends are best.
King James used to call for his old shoes; they were
easiest for his feet.

John Selden (1584-1654)

A83 (Q29) $-40°C = -40°F$.

A84 (Q94) Roy, Tuesday, Terry, Wednesday. The names
appear in alphabetical order, as do the days of the
week.

A85 (Q48) (a) Militarism, (b) Legalisation, (c) Infection, (d)
Protectionism, (e) Commendation, (f) Revelations,
(g) Anarchists, (h) Adversaries, (i) Enormity, (j)
Desecration.

A86 (Q27) Nothing is as easy as it looks. Everything takes
longer than you expect. If anything can go wrong, it
will do so; and always at the worst possible moment.
Murphy's Law
Message keyed: (PRESONGADL) – Press on
regardless.

A87 (Q75) Pam has twins aged 3 and triplets aged 1, i.e.
$3 \times 3 \times 1 \times 1 \times 1 = 3 + 3 + 1 + 1 + 1$. Fran has triplets
aged 2 and twins aged 1, i.e. $2 \times 2 \times 2 \times 1 \times 1 = 2 + 2 + 2 + 1 + 1$.

A88 (Q8) (d) To complete every possible grouping in threes of
the four different symbols.

A89 (Q46a) (i) George Washington, (ii) Abraham Lincoln, (iii)
Herbert Hoover, (iv) Woodrow Wilson, (v) Calvin
Coolidge, (vi) Theodore Roosevelt, (vii) Franklin
Delano Roosevelt.

A90 (Q52) 123   789
            456 or 456 or rotations of same
            789   123

A91 (Q30) 9 below, 10 above. Numbers appearing above the line are spelt with three letters only.

A92 (Q26) Awaiting the sensation of a short sharp shock.
From a cheap and chippy chopper on a big black block.

W. S. Gilbert
(The Mikado)

Word keyed (ALITERON) Alliteration.

A93 (Q4d) Jim wins £26 + £39 + £47 = £112.
Sid wins £12 + £23 + £21 = £56.
Alf wins £15 + £52 + £65 = £132.

A94 (Q25) It is known to many that we need solitude to find ourselves. Perhaps it is not so well known that we need solitude to find our fellows. Even the Saviour is described as reaching mankind through the wilderness.

Havelock Ellis

Message keyed (HIDEANSK) Hide and Seek.

A95 (Q90b) 59.

A96 (Brainbenders for Mentalathletes, Introduction). It is 640 with 16 factors, i.e. $640 - 320 - 160 - 128 - 80 - 64 - 40 - 32 - 20 - 16 - 10 - 8 - 5 - 4 - 2 - 1$.

A97 (Q91) 73. It is spelt with 12 letters. The previous number is spelt with 11 letters etc.

A98 (Q62e) Intricate.

A99 (Q36) The grid should contain 1×1, 2×2, 3×3, 4×4, 5×5, 6×6, 7×7 and 8×8. The missing numbers are, therefore, 5, 6, 8, 8 and all numbers are placed in the grid so that the same number is never horizontally or vertically adjacent.

A100 (Q9) (a) 3. The only one in which the dot could go in both circle and triangle.
(b) 5. The only one in which the dot could go in all three circles.
(c) 2. The only one that is an asymmetrical figure.

(d) 4. The only one in which the two halves of the
square are a mirror image, assuming the dividing
line is a mirror.

(e) 5. The only one in which one dot could go in one
square only and one dot in two square only.

A101 (Q12) Nil. If three are correct then four must be.

A102 (Q54b) 9218
7436
3531
5313

A103 (Q22) Grid One: Across – Jumpy, Thong, Vice.
Down – Quartz, Sky, Fox, Glib, Dew.
Grid Two: Across – Junky, Twigs, Come.
Down – Quartz, Ply, Fib, Shod, Vex.

A104 (Q42) (E) The preceding letters are the vowels extracted
from the question!

A105 (Q96) M ini M
E ffend I
N otio N
S oun D
A xi S

A106 (Q72) Children $2-5-8-11-14-17-20-23-26$
i.e. $2^2(4) + 5^2(25) + 8^2(64) + 11^2(121) + 14^2(196)$
$+ 17^2(289) + 20^2(400) + 23^2(529) + 26^2(676)$
$= 48^2(2304).$

A107 (Q90a) 23.

A108 (Q1a) (i) P. The initial of the planets in order from the
sun. Mercury, Venus, Earth, Mars, Jupiter, Saturn, Uranus,
Neptune, Pluto.
(ii) X. A list of letters in the alphabet which are also Roman
numerals.
(iii) S. The initials of the seven deadly sins: Pride, Wrath, Envy,
Lust, Gluttony, Avarice, Sloth.

A109 (Q78) $9 + 8 + 7 + 6 \div 5 - 4 - 3 + 2 - 1 = 0.$

A110 (Q62a) Telephone.

A111 (Q4c) Liam (i.e. Mail reversed). Dennis Sinned, Delia Ailed and Tessa had an asset.

A112 (Q54a) 5313
6138
4389
3564

A113 (Q2b) 857, 859. Re-arrange the digits of 7731 in every possible way and then divide the resultant number by 9.

A114 (Q6) (e) There are two black arms – one moves through 90° each time and the other through 45°. The dotted line never moves but is covered by the black arms when they coincide with its position.

A115 (Q57a) Aim. All the others contain silent letters.

A116 (Q40) He had already sugared the tea. When the waiter returned with the supposedly fresh cup, he sugared it again and knew it was the original tea as soon as he took the first sip.

A117 (Q33) Answer 604. Turn your calculator upside down and it spells hog!

A118 (Q50b) Transpontine.

A119 (Q3d) (i) Maritime, (ii) Forsaken, (iii) Convened.

A120 (Q69) (a) Hell, (b) Soon, (c) Fresh, (d) Effete, (e) Push, (f) Sever, (g) Alone, (h) Adored, (i) Recite, (j) Elegant, (k) Recreant, (l) Doyen, (m) Loiter, (n) New.

A121 (Q82) For these fellows of infinite tongue, that can rhyme themselves into ladies' favours, they do always reason themselves out again.

King Henry V, vii.162

A122 (Q57b) Sing. All the other words have two pronunciations.

A123 (Q66) They all begin with 'TEN': Tenet, Tentacle, Tenacious, Tench, Tender, Tennis, Tenter, Tenuous, Tenor, Tenantable.

A124 (Q97) Freighter, Yacht, Tanker, Sloop, Trawler, Frigate, Junk, Ketch.

A125 (Q90d) 111.

A126 (Q2d) 72. The number at the top is one quarter of the sum of the two numbers below.

A127 (Q100) (a) Whimsy, (b) Slapstick, (c) Banter, (d) Caricature, (e) Buffoonery, (f) Burlesque, (g) Jocularity, (h) Spoof, (i) Badinage, (j) Satire, (k) Farce, (l) Cartoon, (m) Hoax, (n) Comedy.

A128 (Q88) To fall and not touch a line the card must fall so that the centre of the card falls within the shaded area.

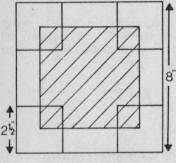 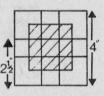

For	Against	For	Against
$30\frac{1}{4}$in^2	$33\frac{3}{4}$in^2	$21\frac{1}{4}$in^2	$13\frac{3}{4}$in^2

In the proportion 1 To 4

	For		Against
Therefore	$30\frac{1}{4}$	–	$33\frac{3}{4}$
	$2\frac{1}{4}$	–	$13\frac{3}{4}$
	$2\frac{1}{4}$	–	$13\frac{3}{4}$
	$2\frac{1}{4}$	–	$13\frac{3}{4}$
	$2\frac{1}{4}$	–	$13\frac{3}{4}$
	$39\frac{1}{4}$		$88\frac{3}{4}$
	$39\frac{1}{4}$		$88\frac{3}{4}$

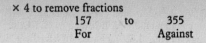

× 4 to remove fractions

157	to	355
For		Against

A129 (Q95) Rain is an anagram of Iran; plane is an anagram of Nepal; chain is an anagram of China.

A130 (Q81a)

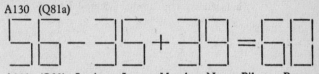

A131 (Q89) Jemimas, Lupus, Macabre, Nacre, Pilaster, Posse, Punnet, Quoin, Azalea, Sept, Velveteen, Toxophilite, Xenon, Yashmak, Ouija, Sepia.

A132 (Q44) Cautioned
Auctioned
Education

A133 (Wind-ups, Introduction) MENSA
MENSE
MEUSE
MOUSE
MOULE
MOULD
WOULD
WORLD

A134 (Q93) 220 and 284; i.e. 220 + 110 + 55 + 44 + 22 + 20 + 11 + 10 + 5 + 4 + 2 + 1 = 504
284 + 142 + 71 + 4 + 2 + 1 = 504

A135 (Q86) Arquebus/Field/Flintlock (All guns)
Atoll/Islet/Key (All islands)
Board/Note/Stone (All can be prefixed with KEY)
Canal/Door/Gun (All have locks)

A136 (Q35) They should tip the barrel onto its edge until the rum reaches the rim. If they can then see part of the bottom of the barrel, the barrel is not half full. If they cannot see part of the bottom of the barrel, it is more than half full.

A137 (Q19) 1.E. Sauces, 1.S.E. Sonata, 1.N.E. Severe, 2.S.
Errata, 2.S.E. Erases, 3.N.E. Agents, 4.E. Era, 4.S.
Etna, 4.S.W. Eves, 4.N.E. Ere, 5.W. Are, 5.S.
Ache, 6.N. Ante, 6.E. Ate, 7.E. Vets, 7.S. Van, 8.E.
Noon, 9.S. Sen, 10.N.E. Gents, 11.S.E. Rases.

A138 (Q59) All the dots except the one on the extreme right are
in orbiting groups around a central dot.

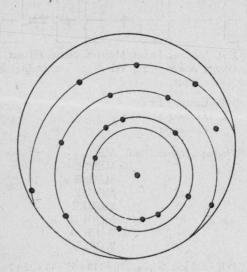